R0083128157

04/2015

PALM BEACH COUNTY
LIBRARY SYSTEM
3650 Summit Boulevard
West Palm Beach. FL 33406-4198

# Scrumptious
# Statistics

Lisa Arias

rourkeeducationalmedia.com

## Before Reading:

## Building Academic Vocabulary and Background Knowledge

Before reading a book, it is important to tap into what your child or students already know about the topic. This will help them develop their vocabulary, increase their reading comprehension, and make connections across the curriculum.

1.  Look at the cover of the book. What will this book be about?
2.  What do you already know about the topic?
3.  Let's study the Table of Contents. What will you learn about in the book's chapters?
4.  What would you like to learn about this topic? Do you think you might learn about it from this book? Why or why not?
5.  Use a reading journal to write about your knowledge of this topic. Record what you already know about the topic and what you hope to learn about the topic.
6.  Read the book.
7.  In your reading journal, record what you learned about the topic and your response to the book.
8.  After reading the book complete the activities below.

### Content Area Vocabulary
*Read the list. What do these words mean?*

cluster
gap
interquartile range
mean
mean absolute deviation
measures of variation
median
mode
outliers
quartiles
symmetry

## After Reading:

## Comprehension and Extension Activity

After reading the book, work on the following questions with your child or students in order to check their level of reading comprehension and content mastery.

1.  Explain the similarities and differences between bar diagrams and histograms. (Summarize)
2.  How is the peak of your display similar to mode? (Asking questions)
3.  What are mean, median, and mode? (Summarize)
4.  What can outliers tell you about your data? (Asking questions))
5.  If you were gathering data, what is a statistical question you would ask? (Text to self connection)

## Extension Activity

Think of a great statistical question. If you need help refer back to the book. Ask several people the same question and record their answers. Create a display by using two of the methods presented in the book. Which display works best for your data? Now present your findings to your parents or friends.

# Table of Contents

# Number Crunching

## Statistics

Statistics have a way of sneaking up in things we do most every day. Statistics can be a simple fact like a sixth grader's favorite subject.

# Data

## Sixth Grader's Favorite Subject

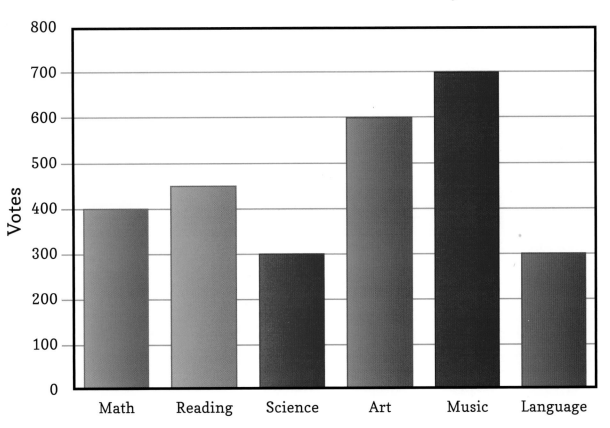

Once the information is collected and organized, it becomes data.

# Statistical Questions

The data you collect is only as good as the questions you ask.

Asking a **statistical question** is what you do
to collect the best data for me and you.

Statistical questions must be written to guarantee
a variety of expected replies that you can see.

Time to get into the groove and see if YOU can prove whether a
question is statistical or not.

| Question | Statistical? | Why? |
| --- | --- | --- |
| How old are you? | No | Lacks variety.<br>Only one possible response. |
| What is the typical age of a middle school student? | Yes | Provides a controlled variety of possible responses.<br>Data can be organized. |
| What is your favorite food? | No | Too many possible responses.<br>Too much variety.<br>Too difficult to organize data. |
| What is your favorite food on the menu? | Yes | Provides a controlled variety of possible responses.<br>Data can be organized. |

Determine if each question asked to your classmates is statistical. Explain your reasoning.

**What is your favorite color?**

**What is your favorite color of the rainbow?**

**How many pets do you have?**

**Do you have a dog or cat?**

**Who is the principal?**

**What month is your birthday in?**

# Statistical Displays

After the data has been collected, just the right display needs to be selected. The display that is picked will do the trick as long as it clearly shows the data you chose.

## Line Graphs

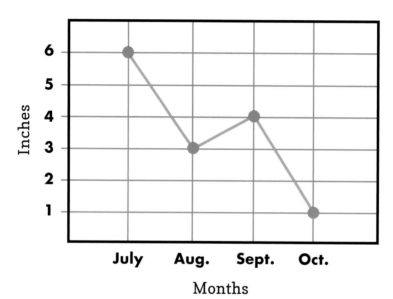

Monthly Rainfall

Line graphs show how data changes over a period of time.

Always connect the dots on a line plot!

# Bar Diagrams

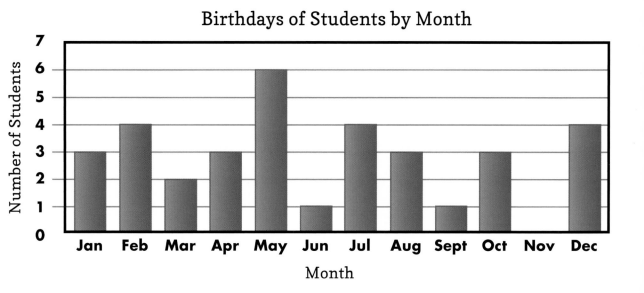

Birthdays of Students by Month

Bar diagrams allow you to easily compare the data that is shared.

# Histograms

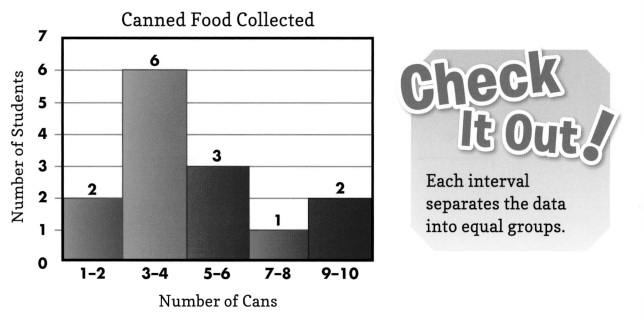

Canned Food Collected

**Check It Out!**

Each interval separates the data into equal groups.

In histograms, the bars touch and the data is grouped using equal **intervals**.

# Line Plots and Dot Plots

Line plots and dot plots use number lines to show the number of times each data value occurs.

Number of Brothers and Sisters

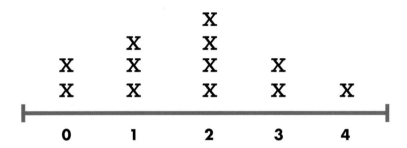

Number of Brothers and Sisters

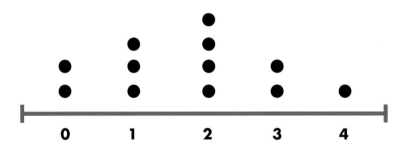

A dot or an X can mark the spot on a line plot.

# Box Plots

Box plots help you to understand
the spread of the data and where things land.

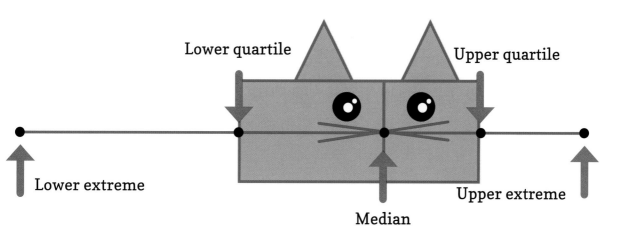

As you can see, box plots are also called box and whiskers plots.

Five special measures help you see the spread of data on a
number line quite conveniently.

# Analyze Data

Once the data has been collected and a display has been selected, analyzing the data will be the key to discovering patterns, trends, and similarities.

The **mean**, **median**, and **mode** are special calculations and measures. Their goal is to discover the best possible number that can be used to describe the data set.

Mean, median, and mode are considered measures of center. Their calculations find the center number of a data set.

# HOW WOULD YOU MEASURE

## 13, 13, 13, 13, 14, 14, 16, 18, 45

# Mean

Wait just yet, the mean is used to find the average of a data set. This measure is used best to describe groups of numbers close in size.

Find the mean.

$$6 + 5 + 3 + 4 + 2 = 20$$

*Add up the numbers in your data set.*

$$20 \div 5 = 4$$

*Divide by how many numbers you added up.*

# Outlier Alert!

**Outliers** are numbers in a set that have values much higher or lower than the rest. Outliers are so extreme that their values are easily seen.

$$6, 5, 3, 25, 2, 4$$

$$139, 98, 110, 12, 125$$

When outliers come out to play,
the usefulness of finding the mean goes away.
This is because outliers cause the mean
to be much higher or lower than what it should seem.

$$6 + 5 + 3 + 25 + 2 + 4 = 45$$

$$45 \div 6 = 7.5$$

7.5 is higher than all of the other numbers.

$$139 + 98 + 110 + 12 + 125 = 484$$

$$484 \div 5 = 96.8$$

96.8 is lower than all of the other numbers.

# Median

If you need to locate the middle value of a data set,
then finding the median is just the right bet.

Order your list of numbers from least to greatest. Count the numbers
on your list.

## 1, 7, ⑧ 14, 26

If the number is odd, the median is the middle number of your list.

Five numbers are on the list. Since five is an odd number, cross
off one number from each end until you reach the median.

When you count the numbers on your list and the number is even, it takes one extra step to locate the median.

1, 2, (3, 5), 17, 18

3 + 5 = 8

8 ÷ 2 = (4)

Median

For the median to be seen, find the mean of the two numbers stuck in the middle.

**Check It Out!**

Outliers are far from the middle and will never affect the median of the data set.

## Mode

The mode is the number in the data that is repeated MOST often.

**12, 14, (15), (15), 14, (15), 16**

Mode is **15**

**MO**de = **M**ost **O**ften

If numbers are not repeated, a data set will have no mode at all.

**1, 4, 5, 7, 12**

**NO** Mode

If there is a tie, you can have more than one mode in a data set.

**12, (14), (15), (15), (14)**

Mode is **14, 15**

Never fear if repeaters are near. The mode is always the number or numbers repeated MOST often.

**2, 4, (5), (5), 4, (5), 2**

Mode is **5**

# Check It Out!

To decide which measure is best, the mode is always a safe bet, if many repeating numbers are in your data set.

# Box and Whisker Plots

Test Scores: **65, 70, 80, 90, 100**

It's time to see how five special measures create box and whisker plots for you and me.

Begin by placing the data on a number line.

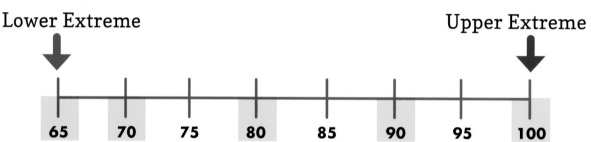

The lowest value becomes the lower extreme and the highest value becomes the upper extreme.

Next, find the median of the data.

Test Scores: **65, 70, 80, 90, 100**

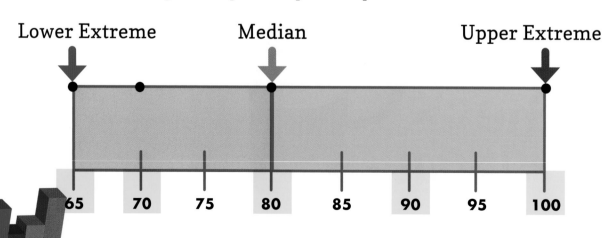

As you can see, the median splits the data into two parts quite effectively. Finally, find the median of each part.

**65, ~~79~~, 80    80, ~~90~~, ~~100~~**

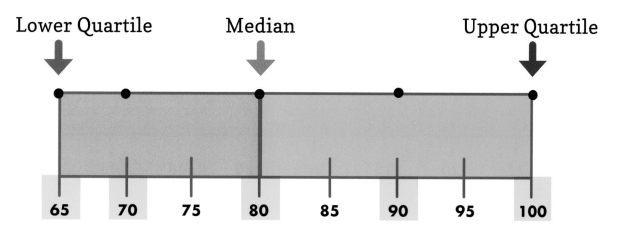

To finish, box off the each measure and draw whiskers to the extremes.

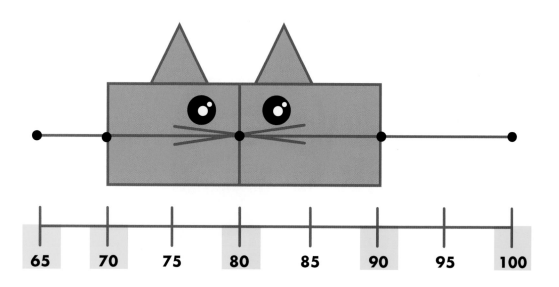

# Interquartile Range

Once each quartile value has been discovered, it is time to analyze the data and find the **interquartile range**. This measure is helpful because it describes the spread of each quartile point.

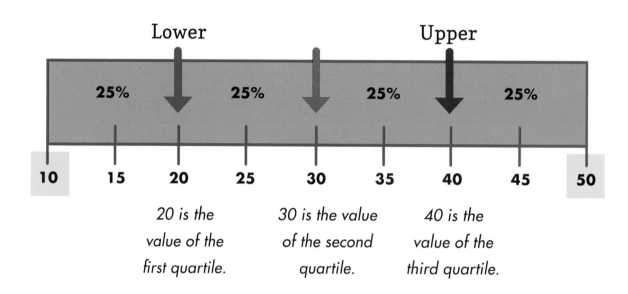

*20 is the value of the first quartile.*

*30 is the value of the second quartile.*

*40 is the value of the third quartile.*

Data Range **50 − 10 = 40**

*Largest Value*

*Lowest Value*

To find the range, subtract the lowest value from the largest value of the data set.

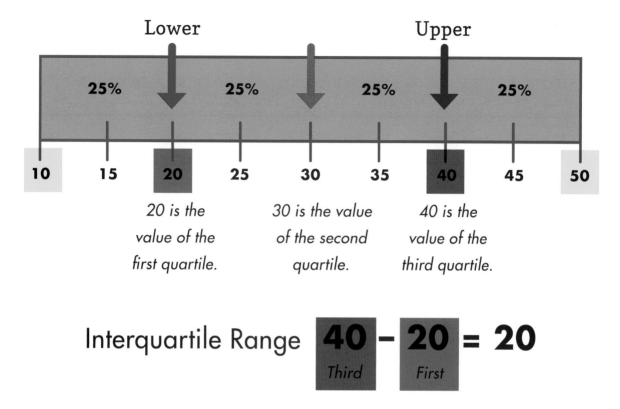

Interquartile Range **40** − **20** = **20**
Third   First

The interquartile range is found by subtracting the first quartile value from the third quartile value.

A low interquartile range shows that that middle data is grouped close to the median of the data set. A high interquartile range shows that the middle data is spread out far from the median of the data set.

# Mean Absolute Deviation

The mean is the average of a data set. The **mean absolute deviation** is the average distance that each value is from the mean.

Follow these steps to find the mean absolute deviation.

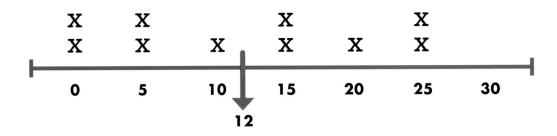

Number of Tokens Earned

*Step 1:*
*Find the mean.*

0
0
5
5
10
15
15
20
25
+25
―――
120

120 ÷ 10 = 12

*Step 2:*

*Find the difference between each value and the mean.*

| | |
|---|---|
| **12 – 0 = 12** | **15 – 12 = 3** |
| **12 – 0 = 12** | **15 – 12 = 3** |
| **12 – 5 = 7** | **20 – 12 = 8** |
| **12 – 5 = 7** | **25 – 12 = 13** |
| **12 – 10 = 2** | **25 – 12 = 13** |

*For values less than the mean: Subtract the value from the mean*

*For values greater than the mean: Subtract the mean from the value*

*Step 3:*
*Find the average*
*of those results.*

$$
\begin{array}{r}
12 \\
12 \\
7 \\
7 \\
2 \\
3 \\
3 \\
8 \\
13 \\
+13 \\
\hline
80
\end{array}
$$

**80 ÷ 10 = 8**

*Step 4: Analyze*

*If the value is large, an outlier may be present or the data is spread out far from the mean.*

*If the value is small, the data is predictable and the values are close to the mean.*

# Shape of Data Distributions

Data is described based on the shape it creates and how it is distributed on a display.

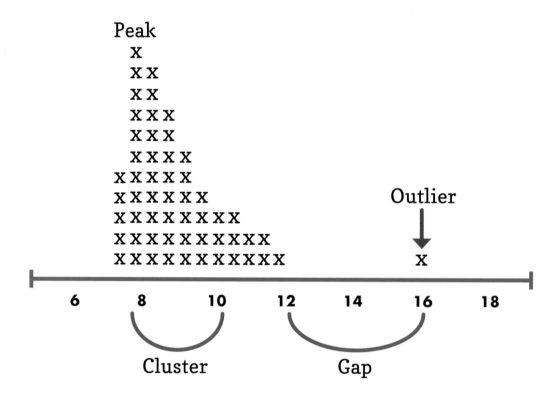

```
Peak
  X
  X X
  X X
  X X X
  X X X
  X X X X
X X X X X
X X X X X X
X X X X X X X
X X X X X X X X
X X X X X X X X X X
```

Outlier
↓
X

```
   6      8      10      12      14      16      18
```

Cluster        Gap

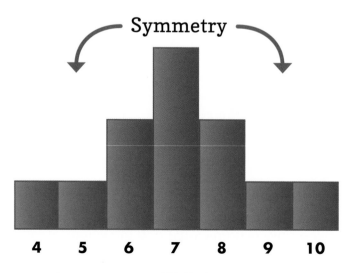

Symmetry

```
   4     5     6     7     8     9     10
```

When analyzing data, it is important to observe the distribution of data. A **cluster** describes data that is concentrated with values grouped closely together.

A **gap** is the part of a graph without any data values.

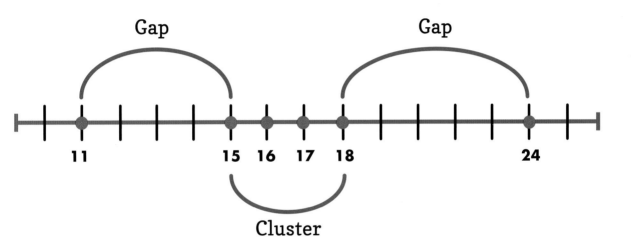

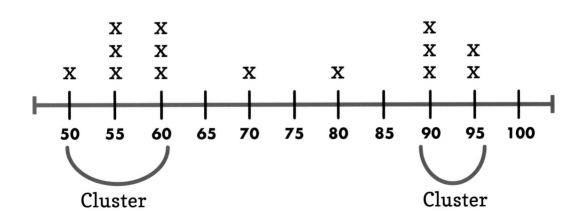

# Peak

The peak is just like the mode and shows the data value that occurs the most.

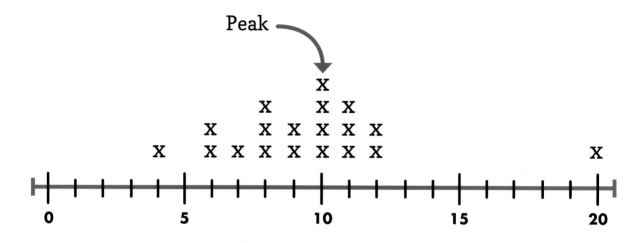

Number of Video Games Students Own

# Symmetry

The **symmetry** of data compares the left and right side of the data.

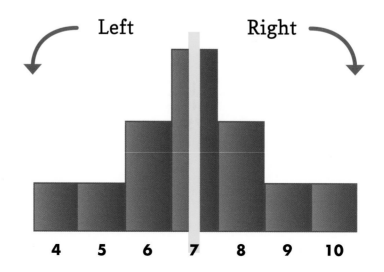

## Shoe Size of 6th Grade Students

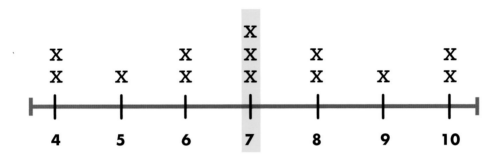

If both sides look the same, the data is symmetric and the mean is the best measure to describe the data.

## Classroom Donations

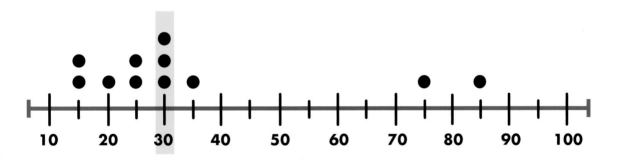

If the data is not symmetric, outliers may be present and the median is the best measure to describe the data.

# Glossary

**cluster** (KLUHSS-tur): data values that are grouped close together

**gap** (GAP): an empty space or interval occurring in a data set

**interquartile range** (in-TER-KWOR-tahyl RAYNJ): the distance between the first and third quartiles of a data set

**mean** (MEEN): the average of a data set

**mean absolute deviation** (MEEN-AB-suh-loot DEE-vee-ay-shuhn): the average distance between each data value and the mean

**measures of variation** (MEZH-urz uv vair-ee-AY-shuhn): shows how data is distributed

**median** (MEE-dee-uhn): the middle number in an ordered set of data

**mode** (MOHD): the number or numbers found most often in a data set

**outliers** (OUT-lye-urz): numbers that are much smaller or larger than the other numbers from the data set

**quartiles** (KWOR-tahyls): measures that separate data into four equal parts

**symmetry** (SIM-uh-tree): identical parts that are separated by a line

# Index

# Websites to Visit

www.aaamath.com/sta818x3.htm

http://files.pbslearningmedia.org/dlos/wnet/dlo2.html

www.bbc.co.uk/bitesize/ks2/maths/data/mode_median_mean_range/play/

# About the Author

Lisa Arias is a math teacher who lives in Tampa, Florida with her husband and two children. Her out-of-the-box thinking and love for math guided her toward becoming an author. She enjoys playing board games and spending time with family and friends.

**Meet The Author!**
www.meetREMauthors.com

www.rourkeeducationalmedia.com

PHOTO CREDITS: Cover © quisp65, macrovector; page 6 © Kali Nine LLC; page 13 © Christopher Futcher

Edited by: Jill Sherman

Cover and Interior design by: Tara Raymo

**Library of Congress PCN Data**

Scrumptious Statistics: Show and Recognize Statistics / Lisa Arias
(Got Math!)
ISBN 978-1-62717-722-1 (hard cover)
ISBN 978-1-62717-844-0 (soft cover)
ISBN 978-1-62717-957-7 (e-Book)
Library of Congress Control Number: 2014935602

Printed in the United States of America, North Mankato, Minnesota

**Also Available as:**